What to doodle? Jr.
EVERYTHING!

Rosie Brooks

DOVER PUBLICATIONS. INC.

Mineola. New York

Bibliographical Note

What to Doodle? Jr. Everything!, first published by Dover Publications, Inc., in 2011, consists of the previously published Dover work *What to Doodle? My Friends* and the new work *What to Doodle? Everyday.*

International Standard Book Number

ISBN-13: 978-0-486-47821-0
ISBN-10: 0-486-47821-1

Manufactured in the United States by Courier Corporation
47821105
www.doverpublications.com

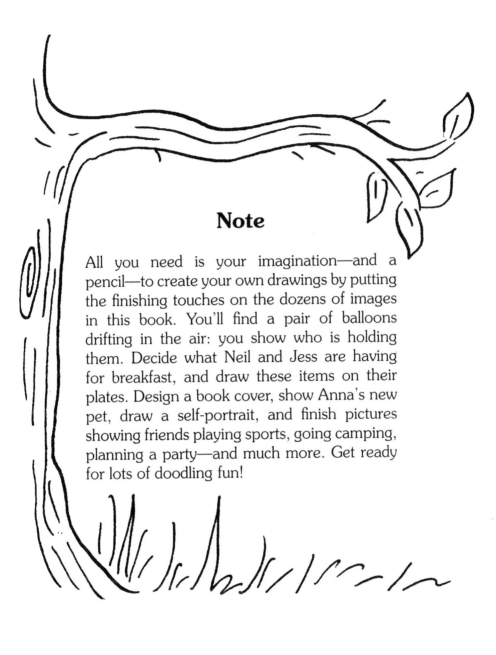

Note

All you need is your imagination—and a pencil—to create your own drawings by putting the finishing touches on the dozens of images in this book. You'll find a pair of balloons drifting in the air: you show who is holding them. Decide what Neil and Jess are having for breakfast, and draw these items on their plates. Design a book cover, show Anna's new pet, draw a self-portrait, and finish pictures showing friends playing sports, going camping, planning a party—and much more. Get ready for lots of doodling fun!

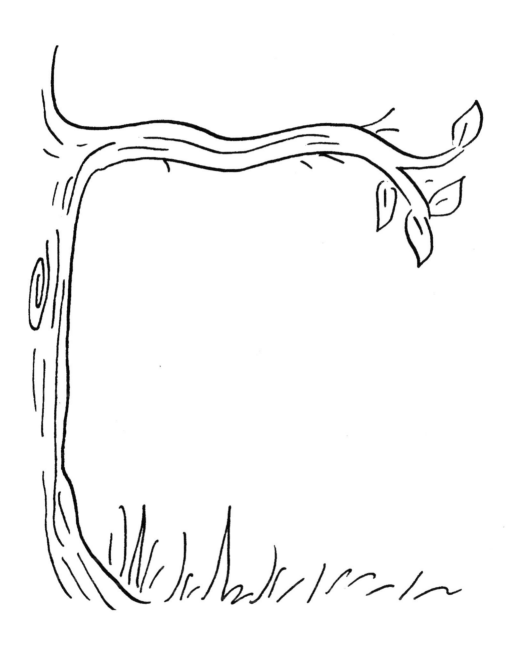

Who is sitting on the branch?

What are Neil and Jess having for breakfast?

How many candles are on the birthday cake?

What type of candy is in the candy jar?

How many people are in the car? Can you draw them?

What is Ben carrying? Can you draw it?

How many labels are on Nick's suitcases?

Can you draw a logo on the sweatshirt?

How many children are hiding in the tent?

Where are the rest of Terry's toys?

How many leaves can you draw on the tree?

What do the girls need to keep dry?

What is Rosie looking at in the shop window?

How many children are climbing the stairs?

What is Simon painting in the picture?

Can you draw Dan's dog?

How many fish can you fit in the fishing net?

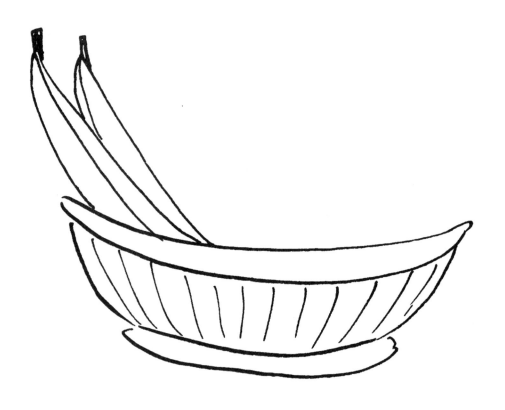

How many different types of fruit can you draw
in the fruit bowl?

36

What is Adam picking from the tree?

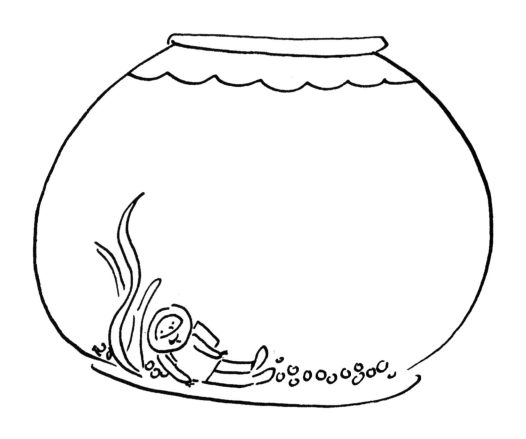

How many goldfish can you draw in the bowl?

What is Chloe carrying in her new vase?

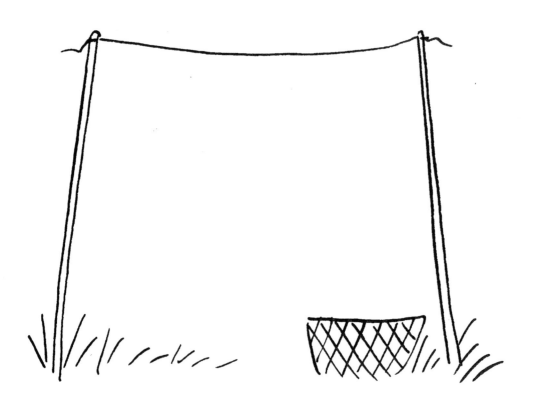

Can you draw some clothes on the clothesline?

What is Clive watering? Can you draw it?

What are the boys looking at?

Can you draw Anna's new pet?

How many ducks can you draw on the pond?

Alex and Jennifer are doing a puzzle. Can you draw it?

Can you draw stripes on the boy's pajamas?

Can you draw what is in the refrigerator?

What are Paul and Joe building in the sand?

Can you draw what Jim and Joanne are playing with?

Can you draw a self-portrait?

What can you draw that goes with a hamburger?

How many eggs can you draw in the hen's nest?

How many windows can you draw on the house?

Can you draw the ice skater?

What is Jane carrying?

What is James mowing with his lawnmower?

What are the mice nibbling at? Can you draw it?

What is Tom looking at in the case at the museum?

How many children are sitting on the couch?

How many spots can you draw on the Dalmatians?

Can you show some beachgoers having fun?

Show Diana and Will's snacks at the movies.

Show what costume you will wear on Halloween.

Susie is a dog-walker. Where are the dogs?

Add a picture of you and your friend to this frame.

Show the game Ellen is playing on her computer.

Where are Fred and Jason's backpacks? Draw them!

What has Justin baked for Charlotte?

How many balloons are George and John holding?

Where are Tom and Charlotte? Finish the picture.

Paul has brought Jane breakfast in bed. Can you draw it?

Who are William and Ryan waving to?

Matt and David are in the candy store. Where is the candy?

What is Luis helping Harvey carry?

What game are Cassie and Chris playing?

Show what Ken and Jamie are climbing on.

Can you draw Max, Martin's favorite pet?

Draw matching patterns on Rosie and Ruth's dresses.

Ian's friend Jonathan is on the swing.
Add him to the scene.

Ian's friend Joanie is on the slide. Can you draw her?

Who is Laura talking to on the phone?
Add this friend to the picture.

What do Philip and Ed need to play tennis?
Finish the scene.

Where have Dan and Ian set up their tent?

What is Alex and Pat's new pet?

What are Oliver and Tim looking at
out of the train window?

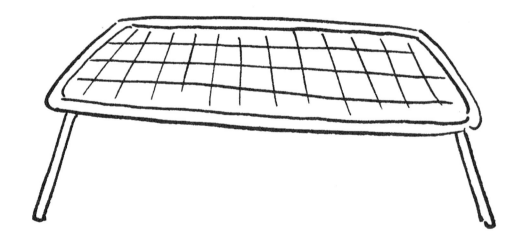

How many friends are playing on the trampoline?
Show them.

Who is hiding in Luke's treehouse?

Who is watching the TV?

Show who has arrived to visit Catherine.

What toppings are Jen and Will having on their pizzas?

Julian and Mike are on the rollercoaster. Can you draw it?

How many children are in the sandbox? Draw them.

Who is acting in the school play?

Who is riding on the back of Bill's scooter?

What can Rory and Matt see underwater?

Who is on the seesaw with Elizabeth? Finish the picture.

How many friends are on the deck of the ship?

To whom is Andy singing?

Can you draw the mountain that Josh and Jim
plan to ski down?

Show who is throwing snowballs at the snowman.

What snacks have Angela and Suzy just gotten
from the food stand?

Who is David talking to through his computer?

Who is holding the ladder so that Daniel can climb up?

How many birds can Ken and Jamie see on the lake?

What are Fred and Jason listening to
with their headphones?

Show the decorations that Miranda and Sue
are putting up for the party.

What is growing in Tom and Rebecca's garden?

What has Miranda brought Jen as a get-well present?

George and Chris are in a band.
Help them play their music by drawing their guitars.

What do Catherine and Becky need to brush their hair?

Alan and Simon are trying on hats. Can you draw them?

Can you draw a lovely pattern on this quilt that
Charlotte and her mother are making?

Finish the painting that Al is showing David
at the museum.

Kevin and Stan would love to go in a spaceship someday.
Add them to the picture.

Where is the ball that Fred and Jason
are playing the game with?

How many friends are on the staircase?
Draw them in so they can go to the park.

Can you draw Jane's friend in the swimming pool?

What have Luis and Harvey spotted in the street outside?

What are Julian and Mike selling at their yard sale?
Finish the picture!